Blue Shoes

A radio adaptation
of Angela Bull's story
by David Calcutt

Illustrated by Jacqui Thomas

Oxford Un

Oxford University Press, Great Clarendon Street, Oxford OX2 6DP

Oxford New York
Athens Auckland Bangkok Bogota Buenos Aires Calcutta
Cape Town Chennai Dar es Salaam Delhi Florence Hong Kong
Istanbul Karachi Kuala Lumpur Madrid Melbourne Mexico City
Mumbai Nairobi Paris São Paulo Singapore Taipei Tokyo
Toronto Warsaw

and associated companies in
Berlin Ibadan

Oxford is a trade mark of Oxford University Press

First published 1998

Adapted from the novel **Blue Shoes** by Angela Bull,
published by Oxford University Press in 1996.

ISBN 0 19 918790 8

Designed by Holbrook Design (Oxford) Limited

Printed in Great Britain

Cast list

There are twelve parts in this play, but you can act it out with a cast of six, if some actors play two or three parts.

Lucy

Mum, Mrs Share, Gran

Anna, Magician, Aunty Sue

Holly, Mrs Robinson

Peter, Assistant

Robin

Note: **Blue Shoes** has been written as a play for radio. This means that everything that happens is only heard and not seen. So as you read, think about:

- how can you use your voice to show how the character you are playing feels
- what sound effects would make the play come alive.

*A shoe shop. An assistant is trying a pair of shoes on Lucy. **Lucy** has already tried several other pairs on. Lucy's **mum** is sitting nearby.*

Assistant   There. How do you like those?

Mum   Oh, they're really nice, Lucy.

Assistant   And they're a very good fit.

Mum   And not too expensive, either.

Assistant   We sell a lot of these. They are very popular.

Mum   Well, Lucy? Do you like them?

Lucy   No. Not really.

Mum   Oh, Lucy! Not again!

Assistant That's all right. I'll go and see if I can find
               something else.

Mum	Thank you. Thank you very much.

Lucy narrates.

Lucy	I'm in a shoe shop with my mum, trying to find a new pair of shoes. I've already tried on five or six pairs, but I don't like any of them. The trouble is, you see, they all look the same. You can see hundreds just like them, up and down the High Street. And I don't want to be the same as everybody else. I want to be different.

*The **assistant** returns with another pair of shoes.*

Assistant	Here we are. Why don't you try these?
Lucy	I'm sorry. I don't like those at all.
Mum	What's wrong with them?
Lucy	They're boring! I hate all these boring shoes!
Mum	You're just being difficult, Lucy! You've got to have some new shoes, so you'd better make your mind up quickly. Otherwise I'll make your mind up for you!

Lucy narrates.

Lucy	I look at them all, lying there in front of me. I really don't want any of them. But I don't know what to do. In a minute my mum will choose a pair, and I'll be stuck with them. I look around the shop. There's nothing! And I'm just about to give up hope, when I see them! And I know right away that they're the shoes for me.
Mum	Well, Lucy? Have you decided?
Lucy	Yes! I want those! I want that pair over there!
Assistant	The ones on the shelf?

Lucy   Yes.

Assistant   I'll bring them over to you, and you can have a
                closer look.

Lucy narrates.

Lucy   They're blue and shiny, with tiny flowers all
                over them. There's nothing else like them in the
                shop. I haven't seen anything like them
                anywhere. They're special, these shoes. Really
                special. And when I try them on, they look just
                right.

Lucy is now wearing the shoes.

Mum   They're a bit fancy. I meant to buy you
               something for every day.

Lucy   But they're lovely, Mum!

Assistant They are pretty.

Lucy   Can I have them? Please. They look great.

Mum   Never mind how they look. How do they feel?

Lucy   (*Quickly*) Really comfortable.

Assistant	Why don't you walk around in them?
Lucy	All right.

Lucy walks around in the shoes.

Mum	Well?
Lucy	Like I said, they're really comfortable.
Mum	You're sure they're not too tight?
Lucy	No!
Mum	All right, then. If you really want them –
Lucy	Thanks, Mum!
Assistant	You're going to take them?
Mum	Yes.
Lucy	And can I wear them for the Christmas Fair this afternoon?
Mum	I suppose so –
Assistant	If you'd just bring the shoes over here, I'll put them in a box –

Lucy	*(To Mum)* Can't I keep them on? I *am* going to the Christmas Fair in them.
Mum	Yes, all right! Anything for a bit of peace and quiet! *(She speaks to the assistant)* Could you wrap her old shoes for me?
Assistant	Of course. Just bring them over to the counter.
Mum	Thank you. *(To Lucy)* Are you sure those are the shoes you want?
Lucy	Yes!
Mum	Right, then. Let's get them bought and paid for, then go and pick up your brothers and sister. The Fair starts in an hour.

> *They go to the counter to pay for the shoes.*

Lucy narrates.

Lucy   So we pay for the shoes, go back to the car, drive home, pick up the rest of the family, and then drive off to school for the Christmas Fair. And all the time, I've got those new blue shoes on my feet, and I can feel just how special they are.

Lucy, Peter, Robin and Holly are now in the school hall, at the Christmas Fair.

Peter   Lucy. Why are you walking funny?

Lucy   What do you mean?

Peter	You're walking funny. Isn't she, Robin?
Robin	I hadn't noticed.
Lucy	I'm not walking funny!
Peter	It's because you've got those new shoes on.
Lucy	What's wrong with them? They're better than your old trainers.
Peter	I like my trainers. They're really good for playing football in.

He pretends to kick a ball and cries out.

It's a goal!

Lucy narrates.

Lucy	I look at his tatty trainers, and at Robin's scuffed shoes, and Holly's brown boots – and then I look at my blue shoes, and I feel just like a princess. And when my friend Anna comes over, she really likes them too.
Anna	I love your shoes, Lucy.
Lucy	They're new. I had them today.

Peter   And they make her walk funny.

Lucy   No, they don't!

Holly   Leave her alone, Peter.

Anna   Come over to Mrs Share's stall, Lucy. She's got a lovely toy dog to give away, if you can guess its name.

*They all cross over to Mrs Share's stall. **Lucy** narrates.*

Lucy   We all go across to the other side of the hall. I have to walk carefully because the hall's crowded, and I don't want to get my shoes scuffed. They make me feel so special, even if they are a little bit tight. But that's only because they're new. I know I'll get used to them once I've worn them for a while.

*They are at the stall now. **Mrs Share** speaks to them.*

Mrs Share   Hello, you lot. Are you going to have a go at guessing the dog's name?

15

Lucy	Yes. Isn't it lovely!
Robin	It's like the ones Aunty Sue makes in her craft shop.
Holly	Aunty Sue *did* make it, didn't she, Mrs Share?
Mrs Share	That's right, she did. Now, who's going to guess first?
Anna	I will.
Mrs Share	Go on, then, Anna. Take a good look at him. Now. What do you think his name is?
Anna	Er... Max. My uncle's got a dog called Max.
Mrs Share	Okay. What about you, Peter?
Peter	White Fang.
Mrs Share	Right. Robin?
Robin	I don't know... Bobbie.
Holly	I'll try Lassie.
Mrs Share	What about you, Lucy?
Lucy	I don't have to guess. I *know* what his name is. It's Scooby-Doo.

Robin   Scooby-Doo?

Lucy   Yes! To rhyme with my blue shoes. Blue shoe –
                Scooby-Doo!

                        *The **children** laugh.*

Holly   How could your shoes have anything to do with
                the dog's name?

Mrs Share   Well, you'll find out later if any of you are right,
                when we call out the prizes at the end.

| **Peter** | I'll tell you something. Whatever its name is, I bet you it's *not* Scooby-Doo! |

Lucy narrates.

| **Lucy** | But he's wrong. Because when the prizes are announced, that *is* the dog's name. And I've won it. And everyone claps when I go up to collect it. |

*All clap as **Lucy** collects the dog.*

Mrs Share	There you are, Lucy. He's all yours. Well done.
Lucy	Thank you.
Robin	How did you do it? How did you know his name?
Peter	She's just lucky.
Lucy	No. It wasn't me that was lucky. It was my shoes.
Holly	Your shoes?
Lucy	Yes. My new shoes. They helped me guess the name. I think they must be lucky.
Holly	That's the first time I've ever heard of a pair of shoes winning a competition. Come on. Let's go and find Mum, and tell her about Scooby-Doo.
	All start to walk out of the hall.
Peter	She can't be right. It can't be her new shoes. Can it?
Holly	Of course not. At least... I don't think so.

*It is later the same day. **Lucy** is in her bedroom at home. She narrates.*

Lucy   Of course, I don't really believe my shoes are lucky. It's just that they're so special, and they make me feel so special. Even so, when I get home, and I'm in my bedroom, I decide to take them off. And I can see that they've rubbed a blister on my big toe. So I decide to put them away in the wardrobe.

Holly *enters Lucy's room.*

Holly   Aren't you keeping your lucky blue shoes on, Lucy?

Lucy   Er, no... they're too nice just to wear around the house. I thought I'd keep them for special occasions.

Holly   Like next week?

Lucy   Next week?

Holly   Dad's taking us to the pantomime.

Lucy   Oh, yes! I'd forgotten! I'm looking forward to that. And that's when I'll wear my new shoes next. At the pantomime.

Holly   You never know, perhaps they'll make
          something special happen to you then, as well.

          ***Holly** goes.*

21

Lucy narrates.

Lucy

So next week comes and I take my new shoes out of the wardrobe, and put them on, ready to go to the pantomime. They feel nearly all right, now. By the time we're at the pantomime, I'm enjoying myself so much I've forgotten that they're still pinching me a bit. And then, what Holly said comes true. Something special does happen, when the magician comes on stage.

We are at the pantomime. The **magician** *is speaking to the audience.*

22

Magician   Now, boys and girls. For my next trick, I want someone to come up here and help me.

Lucy narrates.

Lucy   And everyone's jumping up and waving their hands in the air –

*The **magician** speaks to the audience.*

Magician   How about that little girl there. Yes, you! Come up here. Give her a round of applause, everyone.

*All clap, as **Lucy** narrates.*

Lucy   And the girl he's chosen, the one who everyone's clapping and cheering, the one who's going up on stage to help the magician, is me!

***Robin** speaks to Holly.*

Robin   Why did he choose her? Why's she so lucky?

Holly   Maybe it is those blue shoes.

Lucy narrates.

Lucy   I stand in the middle of the stage, with the whole audience looking at me, and the magician waves his wand, and he begins pulling things out of my pockets –

Magician   Abracadabra – coloured streamers!

Lucy   – and sleeves –

Magician	Hey presto! Fluttering feathers!
Lucy	– and even my ears!
Magician	Fortunata! Glittering beads!
Lucy	And then, he waves his wand once more –
Magician	Izzy-wizzy, let's get busy!
Lucy	– and two huge, blue fans appear out of my shoes!
Magician	Shazam!

Lucy speaks to the magician.

Lucy	How did you do that?

Magician   It's magic. But those shoes of yours helped a bit,
as well, I think. They're very special, and I'm
sure they'll bring you lots of luck.

Lucy narrates.

Lucy   Everyone claps, and I go back to my place. I'm
beginning to wonder now if my shoes *are* lucky
after all. When we get home, it's the only thing
the others can talk about.

27

*We're at home, now, and the **children** are talking.*

Peter   They *must* be lucky. First she won Scooby-Doo, and then she got chosen to go up on stage.

Robin   And she was wearing her blue shoes both times!

Peter   So they *must* be lucky!

Holly   That's silly. Shoes can't be lucky or unlucky. They're just shoes.

***Lucy** narrates.*

Lucy	And now I begin to wonder myself if Peter and Robin are right. Are my shoes lucky? I find the idea quite exciting – but it's a bit scary too. I like my shoes, but I'm not sure I want them to be magical. But there is one thing I'm sure of. I wish they didn't hurt me so much.

Mum calls.

Mum	Lucy! Where are you?

Lucy	In the bathroom, Mum!

Mum	Hurry up and come down. It's your turn to help set the table for tea.

Lucy narrates.

Lucy   I've sneaked into the bathroom to get a plaster to put round my big toe. That blister's very sore now. I'm looking forward to putting my shoes away again, and putting my old trainers back on. I wonder why it is that they feel so much more comfortable? Anyway, when I'm downstairs putting them on, I hear Mum speaking to Aunty Sue on the phone.

We are downstairs, now, and
Mum *is talking on the telephone.*

Mum   You'd almost think they were lucky. First the dog, and then going on stage. I wonder whatever will happen to her next.

> *She pauses as Aunty Sue says something.*

Would you? Yes, I suppose we could. All right, then. Tomorrow. I'd better go, now. They're all waiting to eat. Yes. We'll see you tomorrow, Sue. Bye.

> ***Mum** puts the receiver down, and comes into the living room. She sees Lucy.*

Lucy. That was your Aunty Sue on the phone. I was telling her about those shoes of yours, and she said she'd like to see them. So, we'll all go down and visit her at the craft shop tomorrow. And you can wear your blue shoes.

5

Lucy narrates.

Lucy   Next morning, I put my shoes on again. With the plaster round my big toe, they don't seem to hurt as much as before, so maybe at last they're starting to fit me. I'm feeling much happier when me and Mum and Robin and Peter go down to Aunty Sue's craft shop. And happier still when Aunty Sue tells me how beautiful she thinks my shoes are.

We are in the craft shop now.

Aunty Sue   Let's have a look at these shoes of yours, Lucy. Your mum's been telling me all about them.

Robin   Lucy's lucky shoes.

Aunty Sue   Yes. Your mum did say something about that.

Peter   Whenever she wears them, something good happens to her.

Aunty Sue   Lucky or not, I think Lucy's a very lucky girl to have them. They're beautiful.

Lucy   Thank you.

Aunty Sue   I tell you what, Lucy, I wish I had some shoes like those. Do you know what I'd do with them?

Lucy	Wear them?
Aunty Sue	No. I'd fill them with blue and silver flowers, and hang them on the wall.

Mum	What a good idea, Sue!
Lucy	You can't have these! These are mine!
Mum	All right, Lucy! Aunty Sue didn't say she wanted yours.

Lucy narrates.

Lucy	I feel a bit cross with myself for snapping at Aunty Sue like that. I didn't mean to. It's just that my shoes are starting to hurt again. Then, a customer comes into the shop, and I have the feeling that something is going to happen again.

Mrs Robinson has entered the shop.

Aunty Sue   Hello, Mrs Robinson. How can I help you?

Mrs Robinson   My dog's just had some puppies, and I need a basket for them, Sue.

Aunty Sue   Right. I've got a few here –

Mrs Robinson   It needs to be roomy – there are six of them – and with plenty of cushions.

Aunty Sue   Let's have a look, then.

Aunty Sue lifts down a basket from the shelf.

How about this one?

Mrs Robinson   That looks just right, Sue. How much is it?

Aunty Sue   Five ninety-nine.

Mrs Robinson   I'll take it.

> *Mrs Robinson pays Aunty Sue.*
> *Lucy narrates.*

Lucy   While Mrs Robinson's paying for the basket, Aunty Sue introduces us to her – and that's when something *does* happen.

Mrs Robinson   Those are lovely shoes you're wearing, my dear. I don't think I've ever seen such pretty ones.

Lucy   Thank you.

Mrs Robinson   Tell me, do you like dogs?

Lucy	Yes. But I've only got a toy one.
Mrs Robinson	How would you like a real one?
Lucy	A real one?
Mrs Robinson	I can't keep all these puppies. And I want to find good homes for them. Would you like one of them?
Lucy	I'd love one! Oh, Mum, can I? Please!
Robin	Go on, Mum. Say yes!
Peter	Let's have a real puppy!

Mum	Well – it just so happens that your dad and I have been thinking about getting a dog. So, why not? Yes, you can have one.
Lucy	Thanks, Mum. Thanks, Mrs Robinson.
Mrs Robinson	You're very welcome, my dear. Now, you can't have one straight away, of course. They're too young to leave their mother yet. But you can choose the one you'd like. They're in the car just outside.
Mum	Let's go and have a look, then. *(She speaks to Aunty Sue)* We'll go straight home afterwards, Sue. The children have got to get ready for Gran's Christmas party tonight.
Aunty Sue	All right, then. Bye.
Robin **Lucy** } **Peter**	Bye, Aunty Sue.
Aunty Sue	Bye. I'll see you later at the party.
Mrs Robinson	Thanks for the basket. Have a Happy Christmas, Sue.
Aunty Sue	Same to you, Mrs Robinson.

Mrs Robinson   *(To the children)* Follow me.

> *The **children** and **Mum** follow*
> *Mrs Robinson. As they go, **Robin***
> *speaks.*

Robin   Hey! I know why we're getting a puppy! It's because Lucy's wearing her blue shoes.

Peter   Yes! Let's go to lots of shops. We'll get everything we want then!

> ***Lucy** narrates.*

Lucy   I wish they hadn't said that about my shoes. I'm not sure I *want* my shoes to be lucky. I don't want things to happen to me through some kind of magic. I just want them to happen.

Besides, as I follow the others out to Mrs Robinson's car, the shoes are hurting more than ever, and I just wish I could take them off.

We are out at the car, now, and **Mrs Robinson** *has opened the car door.*

Mrs Robinson   There they are.

Peter   They're fantastic.

Robin   They look just like Lucy's Scooby-Doo.

Mum   They are lovely, aren't they, Lucy?

Lucy   Yes.

Mum   *(To Mrs Robinson)* Rather a handful though, I bet.

Mrs Robinson   Just a bit.

Lucy narrates.

Lucy   The puppies are lying on a beanbag in the back of the car. They all look so lovely, and we can't decide which one to choose. Then, as I'm leaning over and looking at them, one of the puppies squirms out of the heap, rolls across the beanbag, and pushes its nose right into my hand!

Mrs Robinson Well! Will you look at that! The puppy's chosen you, my dear!

Mum   It does look like that, doesn't it?

Mrs Robinson You can have him as soon as he's old enough to leave his mother. And I think I know who his favourite will be.

Mum	*(Quickly)* Oh, I think they'll all be his favourites.

Lucy narrates.

Lucy	I should be happy, but I'm not. Because as we walk away from the car, I see Robin and Peter looking at my shoes, and I hear them mutter to each other.
Peter	We won't all be the puppy's favourite. She will.
Robin	Because of those lucky shoes.

6

Lucy
By the time we get to Gran's for her Christmas party, I'm starting to feel very miserable. I'm having to wear my blue shoes again, and they're hurting my feet, and it's all Peter and Robin and Holly can talk about.

We are at Gran's house now.

Peter
So, you see, Gran, they really are lucky.

Robin
Every time she wears them, something lucky happens to her.

Holly
Even *I'm* beginning to think you two are right.

Gran
They are lovely shoes, Lucy. But aren't they a bit tight?

Lucy
No... Why...?

Gran
You just seemed to be walking as if they hurt you.

Peter
She does that on purpose. She thinks she's walking like a princess.

Lucy
Shut up, Peter!

Gran	Now, now. Don't start arguing. I won't have any arguments at my Christmas party. We'll see if those shoes of yours really are lucky when you play the first game.
Robin	Is it the Treasure Hunt?
Gran	Yes. I've hidden three things in the room – a wooden spoon, a stick of spaghetti, and an elastic band. The first person to find them is the winner. Are you ready? One. Two. Three. Start searching!

> As the **children** search, **Lucy** narrates.

Lucy	We start searching. I concentrate hard on looking for the things Gran has hidden, and hope it will help me forget about my shoes. And I concentrate so hard, that I find them before any of the others do.

We go back to the room.

Holly	What? You've finished already?
Lucy	Yes.
Peter	I bet you haven't found the spaghetti.
Lucy	Yes, I have! The spaghetti was stuck in a picture-frame, the spoon was in a plant-pot, and the elastic band was round the door-knob.
Gran	That's right. Well done, Lucy.
Holly	I've only found the spoon.
Peter	I haven't found anything yet.
Robin	I don't think we should have let Lucy play.
Gran	Why not?

Robin   She's wearing her blue shoes, and they always make her lucky.

Peter   So it's not fair!

Gran   That's silly! Lucy won the game all on her own, didn't you?

Lucy   Yes.

Gran   And here's her prize. A chocolate mouse.

Lucy narrates.

| Lucy | I should be pleased, but I'm not. In fact, I feel like crying. The blue shoes had nothing to do with my winning. It was my sharp eyes that won the game, not my sore feet. But, if I told them, I know they wouldn't believe me. They think my shoes are lucky. But they're not. They're horrible, and they hurt, and I hate them! |

We go back to the room.

| Gran | Now, it's time for the second game. Susan, have you got the tray there? |
| Aunty Sue | Yes, Mum. |

Gran	This is the remembering game. You have two minutes to look at all the objects your Aunty Sue has put on the tray. Then I shall cover it up, and you have to write down as many of the things as you can remember.
Aunty Sue	There's some paper and pencils here to write your lists on.
Gran	And the one who writes the most down is the winner. Ready, everyone? Right. You've got two minutes from now!

Lucy narrates.

Lucy	We all stand round the tray and look at the things. There's a clock and a glass and a tube of toothpaste and a comb, and several other things as well. I've got a good memory, and I know I'll be able to write most of them down. But I don't want to win. So I decide I'm not going to.

Gran	Time's up! Get your papers and start writing.
Peter	I don't see the point. We know who'll win, don't we?
Robin	Yes. The girl with the lucky shoes.
Aunty Sue	That's enough, you two! Lucy, come and sit over here by me.

Lucy narrates.

| Lucy | I sit on the settee and pretend to think, and then I start to write. And I write down the most ridiculous, impossible things I can think of. |

Aunty Sue is watching what Lucy is writing down. She and Lucy speak in low voices.

Aunty Sue	What are you writing down, Lucy?
Lucy	The things on the tray.
Aunty Sue	Fish and chips? The Queen's crown? A Tyrannosaurus?

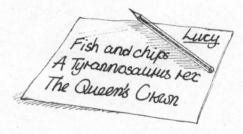

Lucy   I know. The thing is, I don't want to win.

Aunty Sue   Why not?

Lucy   It's my shoes. When I wear them, lucky things happen to me.

Aunty Sue   That's nice, isn't it?

Lucy   No. It's horrible. I won the treasure hunt properly. And Scooby-Doo at the Christmas Fair. But everybody thinks it was because I was wearing the shoes. It feels as if they're taking over.

Aunty Sue	They are very pretty.
Lucy	I know. But – they're too tight!
Gran	That's enough whispering over there! I hope you're not helping her, Susan.
Peter	She won't need help, not with those shoes of hers.
Gran	Time's up! Let me check your lists!

Gran looks at Holly's list.

That's very good, Holly. Eight out of ten.

She looks at Peter's list.

Even better. Nine out of ten.

Peter	What did I forget?
Gran	The safety-pin.

She looks at Lucy's list.

Holly	Here we go. Ten out of ten, I bet.
Gran	No. Not at all. Lucy hasn't got any right!

Peter	None? Her shoes must be wearing out.
Gran	Let's see yours, Robin.

She looks at Robin's list.

Gran	Ten out of ten! You remembered them all! So you're the winner! Here's *your* chocolate mouse.
Robin	Thanks, Gran.
Lucy	Well done, Peter.
Gran	Well, now. That's the games over. Now it's time for the tea.
Holly	Great! I'm really hungry!
Gran	Come on through to the other room, everyone.

*They all go through to the other room. **Lucy** narrates.*

Lucy	I'm glad Robin's won. But the thing that would make me really happy would be not to have to wear these shoes any more. Then, as we go through to have our tea, Aunty Sue takes me to one side.

Aunty Sue   I've had a thought about those shoes of yours, Lucy. Do you remember I said I'd like to make them into a decoration to sell in my shop?

Lucy   Yes.

Aunty Sue   Well, why don't we do a swap? You give me those, and I'll buy you a new pair.

Lucy   Will you? Really?

Aunty Sue   Yes.

Lucy   A new pair of shoes. That will be the luckiest thing of all.

Aunty Sue   Good. It's a deal. We'll go to the High Street tomorrow and you can choose any pair you like.

Lucy narrates.

Lucy   And that's just what we do. Next morning, I'm sitting in the shoe shop, surrounded by different pairs of shoes, trying to decide which ones to have.

We are in the shoe shop now.

Aunty Sue   Well, Lucy? Which of these shoes would you like best? You can have any pair you want – the ones that are the most special.

Lucy narrates.

Lucy　　　　　I look at the shoes. They're all special in their own way, so I choose a pair of green ones with red edging, and try them on.

Aunty Sue　　Would you like those?

Lucy　　　　　Yes, please, Aunty Sue.

Aunty Sue　　You can have them, then. Just have a walk up and down to make sure they fit.

Lucy narrates.

Lucy　　　　　So I walk up and down the shop in my new shoes, and they look really good, and fit just right!

THE END

Treetops Playscripts

Titles in the series include:

Stage 10

The Masked Cleaning Ladies of Om
by John Coldwell;
adapted by David Calcutt
    single: 0 19 918780 0
    pack of 6: 0 19 918781 9

Stupid Trousers
by Susan Gates;
adapted by David Calcutt
    single: 0 19 918782 7
    pack of 6: 0 19 918783 5

Stage 11

Bertha's Secret Battle
by John Coldwell;
adapted by David Calcutt
    single: 0 19 918786 X
    pack of 6: 0 19 918787 8

Bertie Wiggins' Amazing Ears
by David Cox and Erica James;
adapted by David Calcutt
    single: 0 19 918784 3
    pack of 6: 0 19 918785 1

Stage 12

The Lie Detector
by Susan Gates;
adapted by David Calcutt
    single: 0 19 918788 6
    pack of 6: 0 19 918789 4

Blue Shoes
by Angela Bull;
adapted by David Calcutt
    single: 0 19 918790 8
    pack of 6: 0 19 918791 6

Stage 13

The Personality Potion
by Alan MacDonald;
adapted by David Calcutt
    single: 0 19 918792 4
    pack of 6: 0 19 918793 2

Spooky!
by Michaela Morgan;
adapted by David Calcutt
    single: 0 19 918794 0
    pack of 6: 0 19 918795 9

Stage 14

Petey
by Paul Shipton;
adapted by David Calcutt
    single: 0 19 918796 7
    pack of 6: 0 19 918797 5

Climbing in the Dark
adapted from his own novel
by Nick Warburton
    single: 0 19 918798 3
    pack of 6: 0 19 918799 1